YOUR KNOWLEDGE HAS VALUE

Cryptocurrencies in the Industrial Context. The Usage of IOTA in Different Industries

Bibliographic information published by the German National Library:

The German National Library lists this publication in the National Bibliography; detailed bibliographic data are available on the Internet at http://dnb.dnb.de.

ISBN: 9783346925916
This book is also available as an ebook.

© GRIN Publishing GmbH
Trappentreustraße 1
80339 München

Print and binding: Books on Demand GmbH, Norderstedt, Germany
Printed on acid-free paper from responsible sources.

The present work has been carefully prepared. Nevertheless, authors and publishers do not incur liability for the correctness of information, notes, links and advice as well as any printing errors.

GRIN web shop: https://www.grin.com/document/1382639

Crypto-currencies in the industrial context

Economics

Within the framework of the extra-occupational MBA program in Essen

1st Semester

18th January 2019

Table of contents

Index of Figures

List of abbreviations

Business Intelligence	BI
Business-to-Business	B2B
Cross Domain Development Kit	XDC
Internet-of-Things	IoT
Machine-to-Machine	M2M
Mobility as a Service	MaaS
Over the Air Update	OTA
Robert Bosch Venture Capital GmbH	RBVC
Robots as a Service	RaaS
Volkswagen	VW

1 Introduction

"The one thing that's missing, but that will soon be developed, is a reliable e-cash, a method whereby on the internet you can transfer funds from A to B, without A knowing B or B knowing A. That kind of thing will develop on the internet and that will make it even easier for people to use the internet." [1]

When talking about cryptocurrencies, there is one name everybody knows, and this is the epitome and most popular cryptocurrency. This name is Bitcoin. Nowadays there are much more cryptocurrencies available, and not all of them are serious. The purpose of this paper is to have an economical view on cryptocurrencies in the industrial context.

1.1 What is a cryptocurrency?

According to the definition, a cryptocurrency is a digital or virtual currency with a mostly decentralised, shared and cryptographical payment system[2]. The definition of the European Banking Authority is: "Virtual currencies are defined as a digital representation of value that is neither issued by a central bank or public authority nor necessarily attached to a Fiat currency, but is used by natural or legal persons as a means of exchange and can be transferred, stored or traded electronically."[3] If we are talking about Bitcoin there is also always the speech of block chain. Block chain is the technology behind the Bitcoin and must be separated from the cryptocurrency. These are two different things, the block chain and the cryptocurrency. There are cryptocurrencies without a block chain and a block chain without a cryptocurrency[4]. Beside the block chain, there is an alternative technology, called the tangle.

1.1.1 Block chain

In the following the basic function of the block chain will be explained. Because of the reason that the purpose of this paper is not to explain the fundamental function of cryptography, it will only give a simplified impression how the block chain works. It is not

---

[1] *Milton Friedman*, NTU Talks with Milton Friedman, 1999.
[2] See *https://wirtschaftslexikon.gabler.de/definition/kryptowaehrung-54160/version-277214,* accessed on 09.12.2018.
[3] *https://eba.europa.eu/documents/10180/657547/EBA-Op-2014-08+Opinion+on+Virtual+Currencies.pdf,* accessed on 09.12.2018.
[4] See *Thelen, F.*, Frank Thelen - die Autobiographie, 2018, p. 239.

the demand of this paper to go into detail of the distributed ledger technology or other technologies related to the block chain.

As the name already suggests, the block chain is a data chain consist of several blocks. Every transaction is being written into one of those blocks. Each new block is added to the chain.

The function will be explained by an example where one person wants to send money to another Person. The explanation is showing in Figure 1.

Figure 1: How a block chain works

Editor's note: this figure was removed due to copyright issues.

Source: *Financial Times*, Technology: Banks seek the key to blockchain, 2015

The block chain can be seen for everyone at www.blockchain.info.

1.1.2   Tangle

The tangle is designed as a cryptocurrency for the internet-of-things. It shall be the next evolution step of the block chain. Furthermore, it has properties to enable payments between machines, so-called machine-to-machine payments[5]. The same underline conditions as in section 1.1.1 are also valid for this section. It will only give a rough information about the working principle, and not a detailed information about the Directed Acyclic Graph or why it is Quantum Proof.

The tangle system does not consist of single "blocks", as it is the case within the block chain. It consists of transactions. If a user would like to do a transaction, he has to approve two other transactions before. Furthermore, the transactions are handled in parallel[6].

Figure 2: Blockchain vs. Tangle

Editor's note: this figure was removed due to copyright issues.

Source: *IOTA Foundation*, FAQs, 2018

This leads to the fact that the tangle has a much higher transaction speed compared to the block chain. Furthermore, the scalability of the system is given. The more participants are in the system the better, respectively faster, it works[7].

---

[5] See *Serguei Popov*, The Tangle, IOTA Whitepaper, 2018, p. 1.
[6] See *Serguei Popov*, The Tangle, IOTA Whitepaper, 2018, p. 2.
[7] See *https://iotasupport.com/whatisiota.shtml,* accessed on 18.12.2018.

Figure 3: Scalability Tangle vs Blockchain

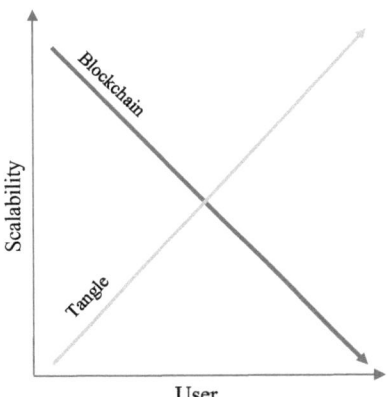

Source: own illustration based on *Rosenberger, P.*, Bitcoin und Blockchain, 2018, p. 51

1.2   Where does the cryptocurrency come from?

It was the 31st October 2008 where an email from Satoshi Nakamoto was sent to a mailing list[8]. Until now it is not sure if Satoshi Nakamoto is single person or a group of people. In the mail, he or the group describes a decentralised payment system using a peer-to-peer network and without the need of a third-party regulation[9]. This is known as the origin of the Bitcoin. But it took two more year to make a transaction payed in Bitcoins. 2010 Laszlo Hanyecz bought two pizzas for 10.000 Bitcoins[10]. The original post and the post of the successful transaction is available on https://bitcointalk.org/index.php?topic=137.0. By using the exchange rate Bitcoin to Euro of today the 09.12.2018 the two pizzas would cost 29.731.800 Euro[11].

1.3   What kind of cryptocurrencies exist (an overview)?

Because of the fact that the "first" cryptocurrency, Bitcoin, is based on an open-source principal, it is easily to adapt for other programmers. This reason leads to the fact that

---

[8] See *https://www.mail-archive.com/cryptography@metzdowd.com/msg10142.html*, accessed on 09.12.2018; See *http://www.metzdowd.com/pipermail/cryptography/2008-October/014810.html*, accessed on 09.12.2018.
[9] See *https://bitcoin.org/bitcoin.pdf*, accessed on 09.12.2018.
[10] See *https://bits.blogs.nytimes.com/2013/12/22/disruptions-betting-on-bitcoin/*, accessed on 09.12.2018.
[11] See *https://www.oanda.com/lang/de/currency/converter/*, accessed on 09.12.2018.

many other cryptocurrencies exists[12]. At this moment, 17.12.2018, 15:42 central european time, there are 2073 different cryptocurrencies listed with a market capitalisation of 109.319.100.057 USD. 55% of this market capitalisation is related to Bitcoin[13]. Because of the huge number of existing cryptocurrencies and their volatility, only the top 10 cryptocurrencies related to the market capitalisation are shown in Figure 4.

Figure 4: Top 10 Cryptocurrencies

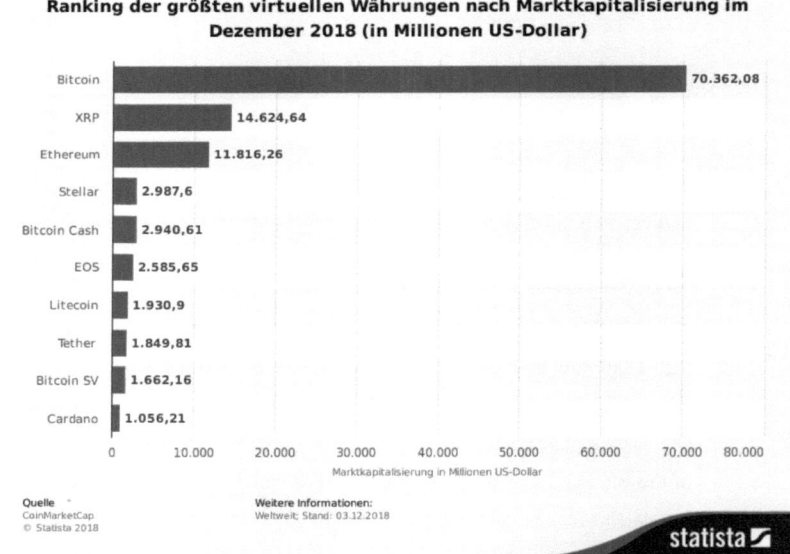

Source: *CoinMarketCap*, Ranking der größten virtuellen Währungen nach Marktkapitalisierung im Dezember 2018 (in Millionen US-Dollar), 2018

As we are going to focus in IOTA later in this paper, IOTA is listed on position 13[14].

2 IOTA as cryptocurrency in the industry

The technology behind IOTA is the tangle. IOTA was founded in December 2015 by David Sønstebø, Sergey Ivancheglo, Dominik Schiener, and Dr. Serguei Popov[15]. IOTA

---

[12] See *Sixt, E.*, Bitcoins und andere dezentrale Transaktionssysteme, 2017, p. 30.

[13] See *https://coinmarketcap.com/all/views/all/*, accessed on 17.12.2018.

[14] See *https://coinmarketcap.com/all/views/all/*, accessed on 17.12.2018.

[15] See *https://iotasupport.com/whatisiota.shtml*, accessed on 18.12.2018.

is developed to be used as a payment system between machines and is focused mainly on the internet-of-things. This machine-to-machine payment is provided without any fees because there are no miners that receive momentary rewards in the network[16]. These payments are called micropayment. Micropayment are payments with very low amount of money what is primarily used in e-commerce. The amount can be that small that it will be uneconomical for card payments[17]. The amount can even be too small to manage for the old-style financial system[18]. It becomes more and more important that not only machines are compatible to each other, but also that they are able pay each other for services[19]. For example, a car can pay the parking garage directly, fuel at the station or the electricity at the charging station for the electrical vehicles without human interaction. This is already reality. On the 08.04.2018 the first charging station where a payment can be done with IOTA was opened[20].

Another important fact is that all IOTA that ever will exist are already produced. The amount is fixed to 2,779,530,283,277,761 and were previously generated in the Genesis Block. This is the reason, as above described, there are no miners.

As a résumé of the pages above the core features of IOTA are:

- High scalability
- Fast transaction
- No transaction fees
- Fixed available amount

2.1 Current situation

Behind IOTA stands the IOTA Foundation. The foundation, with their location in Germany, was established to support the team behind IOTA and the deployment of IOTA[21].

---

[16] See *Serguei Popov*, The Tangle, IOTA Whitepaper, 2018, p. 1 f.
[17] See *https://wirtschaftslexikon.gabler.de/definition/micropayment-37916/version-261345,* accessed on 22.12.2018, 13:40.
[18] See *https://bitcoinj.github.io/working-with-micropayments#introduction,* accessed on 22.12.2018.
[19] See *Serguei Popov*, The Tangle, IOTA Whitepaper, 2018, p. 1.
[20] See *https://blog.iota.org/worlds-first-iota-smart-charging-station-52f9024db788,* accessed on 19.12.2018.
[21] See *https://iotasupport.com/whatisiota.shtml,* accessed on 18.12.2018.

Since 03.11.2017 the foundation is an incorporated non-profit foundation ("gemeinnützige Stiftung"). With this announcement, the first foundation based on cryptocurrency was established in Germany[22].

In contrast to the generalized approach of decentralization when using cryptocurrencies, the most critical point is that IOTA still uses a centralized "coordinator". This coordinator, beside other functions, currently validates the transactions. It is planned to remove the coordinator by the end of 2018 when enough traffic is going through the network[23].

The tangle is virtualized at http://tangle.glumb.de/ and the transactions can be seen at https://thetangle.org/live.

Because of the fast innovation and development in this sector, the description of the current situation now could be obsolete while reading this paper. Anyhow, one of the latest inventions at the IOTA foundation was the IOTA ecosystem. The IOTA ecosystem is a platform where people with different requirements can meet, discuss and learn from each other, or work together on projects related to IOTA technology[24]. Another invention is the IOTA Hub. Because of the unique technology, there are difficulties for external service providers to integrate IOTA in their system. These difficulties will have to be solved by a standardised open-source solution[25].

2.2 Companies investing in IOTA

On November the 28th 2018 David Sønstebø announced the launch of the Data Marketplace. On this decentralised platform, companies can offer and sell their data. At this time several sensor data have been offered on this platform. Right from the beginning a wide range of well-known companies are participating in this marketplace. Among others Bosch, Fujitsu, Schneider Electric and Engie are participants from the first hour[26]. Around 84 companies are taking part on the marketplace now. The complete list can be viewed on https://data.iota.org/#/#participants.

---

[22] See *https://www.winheller.com/fileadmin/redaktion/pressemitteilungen/iota-stiftung-winheller.pdf*, accessed on 19.12.2018; See *https://blog.iota.org/iota-foundation-fb61937c9a7e*, accessed on 19.12.2018.
[23] See *https://www.iota.org/get-started/faqs*, accessed on 18.12.2018.
[24] See *https://ecosystem.iota.org/*, accessed on 20.12.2018.
[25] See *https://blog.iota.org/introducing-iota-hub-5349bb8a29cd*, accessed on 20.12.2018.
[26] See *https://blog.iota.org/iota-data-marketplace-cb6be463ac7f*, accessed on 20.12.2018.

2.2.1 VW and the goal of VW

With 123 production plants worldwide, the Volkswagen Group is one of the leading automobile producers worldwide[27]. On the 9th of June 2018 Johann Jungwirth the Chief Digital Officer released a tweet where he announced a proof of concept for using the IOTA for over the air updates. The proof of concept can be found in Appendix I. According to the experts, more than 250 million connected cars will be on the road by 2020. In the Proof of Concept, Volkswagen announced two goals.

1. "Documentation of over the air update (OTA) process steps on an immutable data storage medium and audit trail, where data integrity can be ensured.

2. Integration of IOTA technology into existing legacy systems to prove interoperability and production readiness" [28].

In the beginning of 2019, VW and IOTA will plan to bring their first product on the market. The "Digital CarPass". The Digital CarPass can provide the history of a vehicle[29].

2.2.2 Fujitsu and the goal of Fujitsu

Fujitsu is the 7th largest company in the branch of information and communication technology worldwide[30]. In April 2018 Fujitsu released an announcement where they explained the benefits of IOTA compared to the block chain[31]. On the 24th of August 2018, Fujitsu released a tweet with their proof of concept [32]. The proof of concept can be found in Appendix II. For Fujitsu the critical factor in the Industry 4.0 is the product quality, supply chain and the audit trail. The goals of Fujitsu are:"

---

[27] See *https://www.volkswagenag.com/en/group/portrait-and-production-plants.html,* accessed on 20.12.2018.
[28] *https://twitter.com/JohannJungwirth/status/1005268618890956800?ref_src=twsrc%5Etfw%7Ctw-camp%5Etweetembed%7Ctwterm%5E1005268618890956800&ref_url=https%3A%2F%2Fcoin-hero.de%2Fiota-und-volkswagen-praesentieren-heute-proof-of-concept-auf-cebit-2018%2F,* accessed on 20.12.2018.
[29] See *https://www.calcalistech.com/ctech/articles/0,7340,L-3741309,00.html,* accessed on 20.12.2018.
[30] See *http://www.fujitsu.com/global/about/corporate/info/index.html,* accessed on 20.12.2018.
[31] See *https://blog.de.fujitsu.com/allgemeines/das-sind-die-vorteile-von-iota-gegenueber-blockchain/,* accessed on 20.12.2018.
[32] See *https://twitter.com/Fujitsu_DE/sta-tus/1032972809427984384/photo/1?ref_src=twsrc%5Etfw%7Ctwcamp%5Etweetembed%7Ctw-term%5E1032972809427984384&ref_url=https%3A%2F%2Fcoin-hero.de%2Ffujitsu-und-iota-zeigen-proof-of-concept-fuer-die-fertigungsindustrie%2F,* accessed on 20.12.2018.

1. To demonstrate an audit trail for a production process with IOTA as an immutable storage medium.
2. To engage with the manufacturing and automotive industry and to drive IOTA-based innovation with Fujitsu´s co-creation approach"[33].

2.2.3   Bosch and the goal of Bosch

With approximately 402.000 employees worldwide, Bosch is a global supplier of technology and services[34]. With a press release on the 19th of December 2017, Robert Bosch Venture Capital GmbH announced that they have bought IOTA token. Robert Bosch Venture Capital GmbH is part of the Bosch Group and invests in start-ups. Dr. Hongquan Jiang, partner at the RBVC, sees in IOTA the potential to be the standard technology for M2M communication[35]. With the Bosch XDK the Bosch Connected Devices and Solutions GmbH, another subsidiary from the Bosch Group, has developed a programmable hardware device what is equipped with several sensors. The gathered data can be sold via the IOTA Marketplace. According to Bosch, the Bosch XDK can be used for any application[36].

In conclusion, Bosch is not focusing on one specific goal compared to the case of VW or Bosch. Bosch wants to provide general solutions for the IoT and Industry 4.0.

3   The effect of using IOTA in the industry

In 2020 the whole IoT-Market in Germany will have at least a turnover of around 50 billion Euro[37]. The business-to-business sector in Germany will have a total turnover generate by the IoT of 24,59 billion Euro.

---

[33] *https://sp.ts.fujitsu.com/dmsp/Publications/public/flyer-proof-of-concenpt-industrie40-audittrail.pdf,* accessed on 20.12.2018.
[34] See *https://www.bosch-presse.de/pressportal/de/en/company-page.html,* accessed on 20.12.2018.
[35] See *https://www.bosch-presse.de/pressportal/de/en/robert-bosch-venture-capital-makes-first-invest-ment-in-distributed-ledger-technology-137411.html,* accessed on 20.12.2018.
[36] See *https://www.bosch-connectivity.com/newsroom/blog/xdk2mam/,* accessed on 20.12.2018.
[37] See *https://www2.deloitte.com/content/dam/Deloitte/de/Documents/technology-media-telecommunica-tions/Deloitte_TMT_Industrielles%20Internet%20der%20Dinge.pdf,* accessed on 17.12.2018.

Figure 5: IoT turnover distribution in Germany by industry in 2020

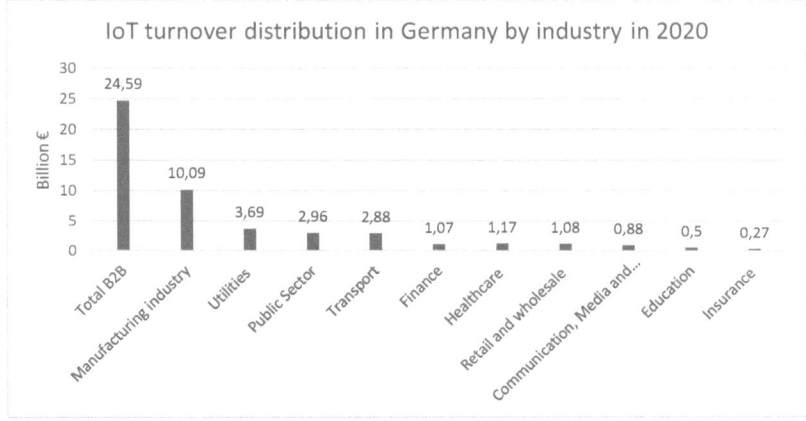

Source: own illustration based on *Deloitte*, Industrielles Internet der Dinge und die Rolle von Telekommunikationsunternehmen, 2018, p. 9

The companies introduced in section 2.2 are from different industry sectors. This shows paradigmatic that the IoT is not only an issue for the IT-sector. Also, especially IOTA as a cryptocurrency for IoT can be an topic for more sectors than the IT branch. Furthermore, it is an issue on all industries sectors, but mainly for the manufacturing industry as shown in Figure 5. Even though that the industrial branches from VW and Fujitsu might be different, there are synergies in the implementation of IOTA. One example is that both companies have transparency as one of their core benefits. To achieve this, they both want to use the immutable data storage of IOTA. While VW is calling it: "

- Establish transparency and digital trust with customers, authorities, and third parties.
- Tamper proof & transparent statistical recording."[38].

Fujitsu has a more generalist approach related to Industry 4.0. In their proof of concept is stated: "

---

[38] *https://twitter.com/JohannJungwirth/status/1005268618890956800?ref_src=twsrc%5Etfw%7Ctw-camp%5Etweetembed%7Ctwterm%5E1005268618890956800&ref_url=https%3A%2F%2Fcoin-hero.de%2Fiota-und-volkswagen-praesentieren-heute-proof-of-concept-auf-cebit-2018%2F,* accessed on 20.12.2018.

- **Transparency:** Improves quality management, after sales processes and customer care management.
- **Trust in Data:** For compliance audits IOTA provides a cryptographical secure source of unified truth.
- **Data Security:** Prevents negative influences such as security breaches, data corruption or fraud."[39]

Even if both companies are following different approaches, both are referring to the transparency and security of IOTA.

All these cases are only a small snapshot on how companies now think of using IOTA in future or working on products which are already realised or will be completed soon.

In the connection to VW and the automotive industry, there are several scenarios thinkable. With the proof of concept from VW, it is not only showing how an over the air update could be realised, but also the whole life cycle, for example service intervals and mileages of a car, could be traceable. More scenarios like the two described in section 2 are imaginable. Cars could pay street charges while travelling on the streets. It is supposable all their parts and usage can be tracked. This data can be used for calculating the insurance or the usage time as billing solutions for car sharing. Trucks could be connected to each other and could use the slipstream of all collected data to reduce the fuel consumption and reward the others for these reduction [40]. These services and scenarios become more and more important. In 2023 there will be around 342,6 million connected cars worldwide[41].

On the other hand, in connection to Fujitsu and Bosch which are more related to the manufacturing industry, there could be a scenario that a manufacture like VW will not own a manufacturing factory anymore. The owner of the robot will lease the work to the producer. This will reduce the downtime of the robot because it could work for several manufactures[42]. As it is seen in the proof of concept from Fujitsu (Appendix II), all steps will be recorded and traceable. Figure 6 shows an example for a conceivable solution to this.

---

[39] *https://sp.ts.fujitsu.com/dmsp/Publications/public/flyer-proof-of-concenpt-industrie40-audittrail.pdf,* accessed on 20.12.2018.
[40] See *https://www.iota.org/verticals/mobility-automotive,* accessed on 22.12.2018.
[41] See *Dennis Becker,* Connected Car Report 2019, 2018, p. 8.
[42] See *https://www.iota.org/verticals/industrial-iot,* accessed on 22.12.2018.

However, there are also other scenarios thinkable. The IOTA Foundation themselves pronounced the following[43]: "

- M2M micropayments
- Reduced costs through predictive maintenance
- Increased efficiency and business opportunities through MaaS/R(obots)aaS
- Smart Supply Chains
- Inventory reduction through BI analysis of data stored in the Tangle
- Improved B2B trust through immutable and transparent record keeping
- Reduction in time and money spent on auditing data"

Figure 6: Production process

Editor's note: this figure was removed due to copyright issues.

Source: *IOTA Foundation*, Industrial IoT, 2018

---

[43] See *https://www.iota.org/verticals/industrial-iot,* accessed on 22.12.2018.

4 Conclusion

The world is in change and the economy as well. No matter if we talk about the IoT turnover in the next years or the outlook for the connected cars in future, there will be a huge amount of data available which has to be handled. No matter if we talk about machine economy where only machines interact with each other without humans or sharing economy where goods and/or services used together respectively shared. The requirements for these economies can be handled by IOTA. Factories will become smarter; robots, whole production lines and cars will be shared. There is no need for a company to have their own complete production line any longer. Machines may communicate directly to machines and pay them according to the factual effort.2016 approximately only 6.382 million devices were connected to the IoT, this number will increase up to roughly 20.415 million devices in 2020[44]. To handle the amount of data and information secured, a fast and reliable IOTA got the required features. How this change will exactly affect our behaviour as humans in the economy cannot be foreseen right now. What can be seen, is that the whole economy will be moved in the direction of a machine economy and sharing economy. With IOTA it is possible to lease everything what is equipped with a chip. Bosch shows that the hardware for this is already available. The cases at VW and Fujitsu show that an industry like the car industry will work together hand in hand with the information and telecommunication industry. Finally, this leads to the conclusion that every company that will operate with the possibilities of this fast-growing environment needs to deal with this in future. No matter if it is a high-tech company or an old-fashion production company.

---

[44] See *https://de.statista.com/statistik/daten/studie/537093/umfrage/anzahl-der-vernetzten-geraete-im-internet-der-dinge-iot-weltweit/*, accessed on 23.12.2018.

Appendixes

Appendix I: Proof of Concept VW

Editor's note: this figure was removed due to copyright issues.

Source: See *Johann Jungwirth*, Johann Jungwirth on Twitter, 2018

Appendix II: Proof of Concept Fujitsu

Editor's note: this figure was removed due to copyright issues.

Source: See *Fujitsu CE*, Fujitsu - Proof-of-Concenpt, 2018

ITM-Checklist

Topics	The sine qua non of success	Comments/Suggestions
Economics	Which macroeconomic relevance is inherent in the topics?	The economic is changing. The growing data and connection between machines will affect the worldwide economy. It will move to a machine economy and sharing economy. This must be adapted on all industries.
Marketing	Which advantages and disadvantages arise out of the suggestions for marketing measures, external impact, and the company's general productivity? Which measures should be taken concerning internal and/ or external Communication?	In the area of marketing, new opportunities arise. If traditional companies adopt the possibilities, they can use the new technology to expand their target group.
Human Resource Management	Which personnel consequences (quantitative or qualitative) result from the suggestions? Which demands does the realization of the suggestions require of the responsible managers? What leadership behavior is expedient?	In the area of human resources, the overhead costs of a company can be reduced because they are not the owner of the manufacturing factory. In case of this the machine by itself can be paid only due its usage period. There is no need to hire temporary working which can be fired

		quickly if the economic went down any more.
Corporate Finance	What criteria have to be considered when choosing appropriate terms of financing? Which risks are existing and what kind of coverage is suggested? How should the influence of external factors be evaluated?	The finance structure of a complete company or even an industry may change. If a car producer does not need to own the production line any longer, can only rent the robot of the line. This may affect the costs of production and can reduce the overhead costs of a company.
Strategic Corporate Management	How is the topic's strategic relevance to be evaluated, especially concerning the aspects of securing existence, competitive advantages, tying up resources, sustainability, and risks?	To be well prepared for the economic and the digital environment in the future, companies should think about their possibilities of using technologies like the IOTA. Strategic decisions should consider the possibilities of these technology to be innovative and stay competitive.
International Business Law	Which legal fields are affected by the suggestions? What has to be arranged in order to create legal security from the company's point of view?	Because of the decentralization of cryptocurrencies, there is no government regulation. The currency IOTA is international, and the technology is tamper-

		proofed. This reduces the risks for a lawsuit.
Value Based Controlling & Int. Accounting	What effects on company key figures can be expected? How does the topic affect the financial statements? What are the consequences?	Because a company could lease their production facilities the property and labour costs will be reduced, on the other hand the cost for rental will raise.
Research Methods	What sources of information should be practised in order to stay up to date in the field of topics?	The topic is highly related to the IoT and changes appears every day. To stay up to date, the available sources on the internet like twitter or the company websites should be used.
Management Decision Making	Which decision criteria should be practised on the choice of alternatives?	The criteria for a decision should not be if the company will implement the technology, it should be in consideration how they implement it.
Digitisation	What are the opportunities and challenges of digitisation? What are the recommendations?	The opportunities seem to be endless. Right now, it might be that there will be no human interface during the interaction between machines.
Business Ethics and	What relevant ethical question may arise in the given context? Which sustainability	In the area of ethics, the question could arise how companies will handle the

Sustainabil-ity	challenges may occur in the given context? Which management measures could be useful to address these potential challenges effectively and efficiently?	huge amount of data that will arise and who will be the owner. If everything and everyone can be followed up in detail, the question of the privacy may come up. The privacy of the humans needs to be protected.

References

Rosenberger, Patrick (Scalability, 2018): Bitcoin und Blockchain, Scalability, Berlin, Heidelberg: Springer Berlin Heidelberg, 2018

Sixt, Elfriede (Transaktionssysteme, 2017): Bitcoins und andere dezentrale Transaktionssysteme: Blockchains als Basis einer Kryptoökonomie, Transaktionssysteme, Wiesbaden: Springer Gabler, 2017

Thelen, Frank (Concept, 2018): Frank Thelen - die Autobiographie: Startup-DNA - hinfallen, aufstehen, die Welt verändern, Concept, Hamburg: Murmann Publishers GmbH, 2018

Online Sources

Asaf Shalev (Blockchain-Enabled, 2018): Volkswagen Sees Blockchain-Enabled Cars in Its Future (2018) https://www.calcalistech.com/ctech/articles/0,7340,L-3741309,00.html [Access 20-12-2018]

Bilton, Nick (Disruptions, 2018): Disruptions: Betting on a Coin With No Realm https://bits.blogs.nytimes.com/2013/12/22/disruptions-betting-on-bitcoin/ [Access 09-12-2018]

bitcoinj (Micropayment, 2018): Working with micropayment channels https://bitcoinj.github.io/working-with-micropayments#introduction [Access 22-12-2018]

Bosch Connected Devices and Solutions GmbH (XDK, 2018): Everything you need to know about IOTA, XDK2MAM and Bosch XDK https://www.bosch-connectivity.com/newsroom/blog/xdk2mam/ [Access 20-12-2018]

CoinMarketCap (CoinMarketCap, 2018): All Cryptocurrencies | CoinMarketCap (2018) https://coinmarketcap.com/all/views/all/ [Access 17-12-2018]

— (Marktkapitalisierung, 2018): Ranking der größten virtuellen Währungen nach Marktkapitalisierung im Dezember 2018 (in Millionen US-Dollar) (2018) https://coinmarketcap.com/ [Access 17-12-2018]

Deloitte (IoT, 2018): Industrielles Internet der Dinge und die Rolle von Telekommunikationsunternehmen (2018) https://www2.deloitte.com/content/dam/Deloi-
tte/de/Documents/technology-media-
telecommunications/Deloitte_TMT_Industrielles%20Inter-
net%20der%20Dinge.pdf [Access 17-12-2018]

Dennis Becker (Connected, 2018): Connected Car Report 2019: Statista Digital Market
Outlook – Market Report, Connected 2018 (2018) https://de.statista.com/statis-
tik/studie/id/43051/dokument/digital-market-outlook-connected-car-market-re-
port/ [Access 22-12-2018]

The European Banking Authority (virtual currencies, 2014): EBA Opinion on 'virtual
currencies' (2014) https://eba.europa.eu/documents/10180/657547/EBA-Op-
2014-08+Opinion+on+Virtual+Currencies.pdf [Access 09-12-2018]

Financial Times (Technology, 2015): Technology: Banks seek the key to blockchain
(2015) https://www.ft.com/content/eb1f8256-7b4b-11e5-a1fe-567b37f80b64 [Ac-
cess 18-12-2018]

Fujitsu CE (Indutry 4.0, 2018): Fujitsu - Proof-of-Concenpt: Indutry 4.0 - Audit Trail
(2018) https://sp.ts.fujitsu.com/dmsp/Publications/public/flyer-proof-of-concenpt-
industrie40-audittrail.pdf [Access 20-12-2018]

— (Produktqualität, 2018): Fujitsu CE on Twitter https://twitter.com/Fujitsu_DE/sta-
tus/1032972809427984384/photo/1?ref_src=twsrc%5Etfw%7Ctw-
camp%5Etweetembed%7Ctwterm%5E1032972809427984384&ref_url=https%3
A%2F%2Fcoin-hero.de%2Ffujitsu-und-iota-zeigen-proof-of-concept-fuer-die-fer-
tigungsindustrie%2F [Access 20-12-2018]

Fujitsu Limited (Glance, 2018): Fujitsu at a Glance - Fujitsu Global (2018)
http://www.fujitsu.com/global/about/corporate/info/index.html [Access 20-12-
2018]

Gartner (Geräte, 2017): Prognose zur Anzahl der vernetzten Geräte im Internet der
Dinge (IoT) weltweit in den Jahren 2016 bis 2020 (in Millionen Einheiten) (2017)
https://de.statista.com/statistik/daten/studie/537093/umfrage/anzahl-der-vernetz-
ten-geraete-im-internet-der-dinge-iot-weltweit/ [Access 23-12-2018]

Greve, Edward (Hub, 2018): Introducing: IOTA Hub! – IOTA (2018)
https://blog.iota.org/introducing-iota-hub-5349bb8a29cd [Access 20-12-2018]

IOTA Foundation (FAQ, 2018): FAQs (2018) https://www.iota.org/get-started/faqs
[Access 18-12-2018]

— (Industrial, 2018): Industrial IoT (2018) https://www.iota.org/verticals/industrial-iot
[Access 22-12-2018]

— (Ecosystem, 2018): IOTA Ecosystem (2018) https://ecosystem.iota.org/ [Access 20-
12-2018]

— (Mobility, 2018): Mobility & Automotive (2018) https://www.iota.org/verticals/mo-
bility-automotive [Access 22-12-2018]

IOTA Support (IOTA, 2018): IOTA Support - what is IOTA? (2018) https://iotasup-
port.com/whatisiota.shtml [Access 18-12-2018]

Johann Jungwirth (over-the-air, 2018): Johann Jungwirth on Twitter (8. Juni 2018)
https://twitter.com/JohannJungwirth/sta-
tus/1005268618890956800?ref_src=twsrc%5Etfw%7Ctwcamp%5Etweetem-
bed%7Ctwterm%5E1005268618890956800&ref_url=https%3A%2F%2Fcoin-
hero.de%2Fiota-und-volkswagen-praesentieren-heute-proof-of-concept-auf-cebit-
2018%2F [Access 20-12-2018]

mail-archive.com (Bitcoin, 2009): Bitcoin v0.1 released (2009) https://www.mail-ar-
chive.com/cryptography@metzdowd.com/msg10142.html [Access 09-12-2018]

metzdowd (P2P, 2011): Bitcoin P2P e-cash paper
http://www.metzdowd.com/pipermail/cryptography/2008-October/014810.html
[Access 09-12-2018]

Milton Friedman (National Taxpayers Union, 1999): NTU Talks with Milton Friedman,
Interview vom 01. March 1999 in , National Taxpayers Union
https://www.youtube.com/watch?v=6MnQJFEVY7s [Access 24-12-2018]

OANDA (exchange rate, 2018): Währungsrechner | Devisenkurse | OANDA
https://www.oanda.com/lang/de/currency/converter/ [Access 09-12-2018]

Prof. Dr. Oliver Bendel (Kryptowährung, 2018): Definition: Kryptowährung
https://wirtschaftslexikon.gabler.de/definition/kryptowaehrung-54160/version-
277214 [Access 09-12-2018]

Prof. Dr. Tobias Kollmann (Micropayment, 2018): Definition: Micropayment
https://wirtschaftslexikon.gabler.de/definition/micropayment-37916/version-
261345 [Access 22-12-2018]

Robert Bosch GmbH (Bosch, 2018): Bosch Company https://www.bosch-
presse.de/pressportal/de/en/company-page.html [Access 20-12-2018]

Robert Bosch Venture Capital GmbH (RBVC, 2018): Robert Bosch Venture Capital
makes first investment in distributed ledger technology https://www.bosch-
presse.de/pressportal/de/en/robert-bosch-venture-capital-makes-first-investment-
in-distributed-ledger-technology-137411.html [Access 20-12-2018]

Satoshi Nakamoto (Electronic Cash, 2008): Bitcoin: A Peer-to-Peer Electronic Cash
System https://bitcoin.org/bitcoin.pdf [Access 09-12-2018]

Serguei Popov (Tangle, 2018): The Tangle, IOTA Whitepaper, Tangle 2018 https://as-
sets.ctfas-
sets.net/r1dr6vzfxhev/2t4uxvsIqk0EUau6g2sw0g/45eae33637ca92f85dd9f4a3a21
8e1ec/iota1_4_3.pdf [Access 18-12-2018]

Simone Selbmannam (Benefits, 2018): Das sind die Vorteile von IOTA gegenüber
Blockchain https://blog.de.fujitsu.com/allgemeines/das-sind-die-vorteile-von-iota-
gegenueber-blockchain/ [Access 20-12-2018]

Sønstebø, David (Marketplace, 2017): IOTA Data Marketplace – IOTA (2017)
https://blog.iota.org/iota-data-marketplace-cb6be463ac7f [Access 20-12-2018]

— (Foundation, 2017): IOTA Foundation – IOTA (2017) https://blog.iota.org/iota-foun-
dation-fb61937c9a7e [Access 19-12-2018]

van den Brink, Harm (Charging, 2018): World's first IOTA Smart Charging Station –
IOTA (2018) https://blog.iota.org/worlds-first-iota-smart-charging-station-
52f9024db788 [Access 19-12-2018]

Volkswagen AG (VW, 2018): Portrait & Production Plants | Volkswagen Group
https://www.volkswagenag.com/en/group/portrait-and-production-plants.html
[Access 20-12-2018]

WINHELLER (Stiftung, 2017): Erste Krypto-Stiftung Deutschlands gegründet
https://www.winheller.com/fileadmin/redaktion/pressemitteilungen/iota-stiftung-
winheller.pdf [Access 19-12-2018]

YOUR KNOWLEDGE HAS VALUE